The Little Book of Silly Rhymes & Odd Verses

Ian Hooper

Copyright

Text copyright © Ian Hooper, 2016
Illustrations copyright © Alison Mutton 2016

Published 2022, by Leschenault Press
Leschenault, Western Australia

ISBN: 9781922670809 - Paperback Edition
All rights reserved.

The right of Ian Hooper to be identified as author of this Work has been asserted by him in accordance with sections 77 and 78 of the Copyright, Designs and Patents Act 1988.

No part of this publication may be reproduced, stored in retrieval system, copied in any form or by any means, electronic, mechanical, photocopying, recording or otherwise transmitted without written permission from the publisher. You must not circulate this book in any format.

Cover image based on a photograph by Mary and Angus Hogg (2011) Under Creative Commons Attribution-Share Alike 2.0. Appearance of Sam McLarnon loosely based on a photo by Argyll Images, used with permission.

Dedication

To all who have endured my rhymes
&
to you,
'cos you're about to.

And to my mum
My greatest hero and best supporter

Forward

Thanks to all the many, many people who over the years have encouraged me, or indeed requested me, to write a poem or two. Also, my most sincere thanks to Alison for the marvellous illustrations.

As you make your way through this little book you might want to read the verses aloud, as that was what they were intended for. Just occasionally you might need a twang of a Northern Irish accent to make *eight* rhyme with *mate*. But, you'll figure it out.

This is not meant to be a literary marvel. It is full of silly stanzas and passable poetry, but I trust some of them will make you smile and some might make you think.

And yes, of course I still take requests.

Regards
Ian
March 2016

I decided, after a few years, to reissue this under my own name, so as to differentiate it and my other poetry books from my crime thrillers. So if you're reading this version, there's no real changes from this to the first edition. Well, except this bit and the dedication. And, ah, go on, have an extra wee rhyme to indulge me. For stuff happened in the last 6 years. Ian, 2022.

She was clever, she was smart, she could dance and loved her art
She was stylish and sublime, mastered diction all the time
She was fearless, never bowed, never victim, never cowed
She was warm and kind and free, but for all of that, to me
She was my friend, my chum; my strength, my hope, my Mum.

Contents

The poems are listed alphabetically in the book, but break into four main themes:

Silly Rhymes

A Tale of Two Drawers	8
Birthday Wishes	10
Delivery	13
Divinity	16
Happy Birthday (Of course I remembered)	19
Love And Romance Never Ends	26
Self-reflections	42
Southern Santa	43
Sunday Mornings	44
There's something not right with my tummy	47
Weekday Jam	53
What do you get a Chihuahua for Christmas?	55

A Little More Serious

Born of Fragments	12
Latharna's Race	22
Life's Gallery	25
Lover's Smile	27
One Sun	34
Occasions	35
Parallels	36
River Paths	41
The Fall	45
The Nine	46
Wind in city valleys	54

A Lot More Serious

Distance	14
Ease	17
Multitudes of Indifference	31
Next Time	33
Princess Victoria (Women and Children First)	39
Revolve	40
View from a Bus Window	48

Of War and Remembrance

Glistening Silos	18
In Belfast last night...	20
Make It Royal	28
Mark Armstrong, Private 1319, 13th Battalion, East Yorkshire Regiment	30
Poppy Wreaths Are Laid	37
Waving Goodbye	51

About the Author	56
Extras	56
Also by Ian	57

Silly Rhymes
&
Odd Verses

A Tale of Two Drawers

When I was little, no more than a tot,
I'd skip home from school,
show my Mum what I'd got.
A simple gold star, the teacher so kind.
My Mum, full of smiles,
thought the teacher was blind.

My Mother, an artist,
her brushstrokes so fine,
could sketch out a scene
with a curve and a line.
But try as I might to follow her lead,
my genes, so defective,
just wouldn't take heed.

But beautiful Mum held my picture with pride.
She knew how to comment and never once lied.
She merely spoke truth, with a measure of tact,
and she focussed upon, the one simple fact.

"I do love your suns, they are always so bright,
and round and inviting and shining with light.
The beautiful orb hanging up in the sky."

My Mother, so clever, not one word a lie.
I'd beam back at Mum, so content with my life,
and as I grew older, took an artistic wife.
One day they both spoke of the boy that I was.
My wife shook her head, said I'd been a lost cause.

My Mum laughed aloud and spoke of the sun
that appeared on each picture that I'd ever done.
My wife laughed along as she heard my Mum say,

"At least I could hold them around the right way.
Without the small glow, so yellow so bright,
I'd never have known I was holding it right.
No way to work out where the bottom should be,
no way to give clues to what I should see.
But with the sun shining on each scene below,
I could hazard a guess at the content on show."

Ah how they laughed and teased me for fun.
My two women drawers, neither needing a sun.

Birthday Wishes

It's my mate's birthday, he's looking well
I know he's older, but you couldn't tell
For he's happy and settled, content with his life
Has beautiful kids and a marvellous wife
All in all he has done it, that thing that's so rare
Grown up, become adult,
kept most of his hair.

He's into his forties, but he's fit as a fiddle
Not for him a beer gut, no spread round the middle
Not to say that he doesn't indulge in a few
But he has a regime, that he sticks to like glue
He cycles you see, on a bike that's so light
It weighs less than the mars bars,
I eat every night.

So while I am gaining the pounds here and there
He is out cycling, enjoying the air
His marvellous attitude, is quite inspiring
But to be perfectly honest, the thought of it's tiring
I would love to do it, I'd considered before
But there's one major aspect,
I can't seem to ignore.

It's silly I know, and I just shouldn't care
But no middle aged man should buy Lycra to wear
Clinging and sticking to all of their curves
I see them ride by and they get on my nerves
I know it is sexist to think or to say
But great looking women,
would make it okay.

But they're not, these are MAMILs, a phrase that is new
I probably better explain it to you
Middle Aged Men In Lycra it means
And the rise of this beast continues it seems
Unabashed, undeterred, riding bikes that are light
And scaring old ladies,
with garments so tight.

But when that's all said, and dusted and done
I know my mate does it for fitness and fun
He loves his wee bike, and thrills to the ride
And issues of Lycra should be left to one side
For today it's his birthday and I'd just like to say,
May you have open roads,
as you cycle away.

Born of Fragments

Only when the sun sets and the cuckoo flies o'er the winding river
When the mist clears from the vista to reveal the seven shining stars
Only then will I look toward you and realize
You are not mine.

If that day comes and signs align in heavenly azure
Then my heart will break and scatter to the winds
The remnants of its beat cascading to the water
Echoing to the world that you are perfect.

Delivery

Mummy shouted at Daddy
Daddy smiled his smile.
Mummy swore at Daddy
All the laborious while.

Daddy held her hand
And vowed he loved her still.
Mummy said his chance of sex
After this was nil.

Daddy nodded thoughtfully
Mummy said it was his fault.
Then threatened to cut his manhood off
And rub the wound with salt.

But then the test was over
And a peace descended down.
Mummy said she hadn't meant
For him to leave the town.

The words she said were only words
Emotions in a whirl.
As Mummy and Daddy kissed again
And beheld their little girl.

Distance

I see you through technology,
the distance closed by light.
From over half a world away
I hold you in my sight.
I watch you as you talk to me
my mother, always there.
Yet the heartache that I feel tonight
is difficult to bear.

For you look like her,
you speak like her,
your eyes are full of life.
Your spirit so unbroken,
your wit, the sharpest knife.

The memories of your girlhood days,
those years left far behind
are fresh and sharp and focused,
vibrant colours in your mind.

I know I'm blessed to have you,
when so many are forlorn.
Those adults who are orphans,
no parents, save to mourn.
While I can still hold on to you
like the child I'll always be.
For the years have made no impact,
on that bond twixt you and me.

Yet now my heart is breaking
though my tears are kept at bay,
as you recall your history
yet know little of today.
The simple tasks confuse you,

in a fog that seems to bind
and I dread the time that's coming,
when I'm a stranger to your mind.
Shall you ask me who I am and why
I've come to visit here?
And will I lie, conceal the hurt
and wipe away a tear?

But that day; it hasn't come yet.
For now I'm still your child
and the fact a God so loving
causes heartache makes me wild
with an anger that consumes me
and a rage that hurts my soul
and a knowledge of futility
that takes a heavy toll.

Yet if I let that anger
pull the focus from my love,
I will never truly see you
as the angel from above
that you will surely be to me
when you have slipped away,
from the sadness and the loss of you,
... that the mind brings with decay.

Divinity

Eloquence, it's such a skill
To find the words
To fit the bill
To utter forth, to talk with ease
To annunciate
And never freeze.

But lack of diction, frustrating pauses
That's the thing
That often causes
Lousy language, profane and vile
And so I ask
For you to smile
And accept the *"Sorry"*, that is mine
For to swear is human,
To forgive divine.

Ease

In each twilight breath of mad world rushing
I sit and watch dying millions with consummate ease.
Sorrowful wailing plumes of smoke

Flag waving tower blocks collapsing into famine
Hatred etched on a million hearts lasting generations
Unforgiving in their parent's brother's sister's children's death throes
My herald flicking to faraway places with faraway problems

Flies settling ungraciously on bodies bloated, faces crusted
Children eyeing life, furtive passers-by too scared to stop
Bread, bombs, shells, milk

As twilight decays to darkness
I sit and watch rising shares with consummate ease.
Rainy weather with annoyance, fickle laws with frustration
Political platitudes with resignation
And death flies off to bother people who are not mine.
Rarely am I prone to find a tear of conscience and when I do
I write to exorcise my mind
From the futility of extremism, the futility of inaction,
My inaction and it feels, it always feels,
Too little, too late, a cheat.

An easy cheat.

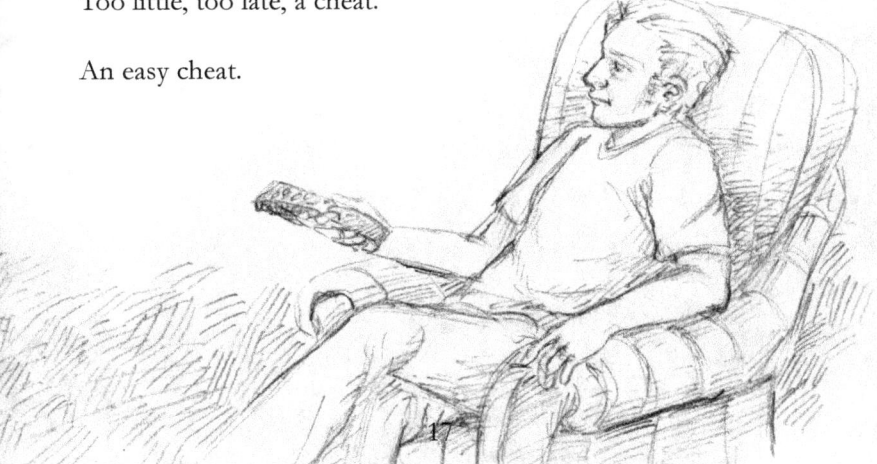

Glistening Silos

We spent years waiting.
Just waiting. In readiness.
Underground with vented angst
in unadorned surrounds.
Waiting for the Bear to turn
balanced on four minute pivots.
Air forced up through shining steel.

Walls fell and worlds newly ordered
moved us onwards.
No more to drill, no more to shine
the polished spheres that topped our world
and rust claimed the brightness.
A redness unexpected.

Now yellow blooms in wildness spread
and trees reach high for turquoise skies.
Yet still in this place, unafraid
the wolf adorned with shadowed crown
stalks the memories of wanton death.
Which never came, nor never left.

Happy Birthday
(Of course I remembered)

Happy Birthday,
Congrats
Good luck and well done
Best wishes,
Regards,
Here's to a great one.

It's not even six and I've done a good deed
I'm not out of bed yet, but there's really no need
For I have a tablet that I don't take or swallow
That allows me to surf, to like and to follow
I can tweet like a bird, or chat nice and snappy
I can flicker and tumble, it makes me so happy
But the best thing it does, which I think is great
Is show me your birthday, so I'm never late
With the greetings and tidings I wish to convey
For let's face it, there's no chance, a card's on its way.

So hooray, Happy Birthday my wonderful friend
May you get enough mentions your name starts to trend
May your selfie go viral, for it's such a great look
And of course I'd remember without my Facebook?

In Belfast last night...

In Belfast last night, another soldier died
And I was standing by his side,
His blood and brains, upon my chest
The reaper's laugh in cruel jest.

Another name on marble lists
And terrorists will clinch their fists
And shouts of freedom ring out again,
But no one feels his family's pain.

In Ulster, he's forgotten; just another Brit dead.
Eighteen years old the newspaper's said,
But no one remembers his face or his name, for all of these killings now sound just the same.

A mother in black stands by his grave side.
We comrades, are there recalling his pride.
A volley of shots reports through the grief, and like his short life, the tribute's too brief.

Then a bomb in a waste-basket at Kings Cross station
Awakens the wrath of this sleeping nation.
"Stiff upper lip, we'll never give in, we've been blitzed before and we didn't lose then."

So newspapers fill with this latest outrage,
With pictures of wastepaper bins on the page.
And pledges from Government to fight the good fight, whilst everyone goes home and sleeps sound at night.

But young men are dying in streets over there.
And commuters in England ask,
"Streets over where?"
"Oh Northern Ireland, I don't understand, and I've no wish to learn thanks; other matters at hand."

"It's not my concern they can do as they like."
"I think we should leave them alone to their fight."

But if you look past the media machine
The drums and the marches, the orange, the green.
The people who walk along Belfast's Broadway, are people like
you at the end of the day.

And the soldiers who die in a terrorist bomb
Are the same make of men who fell at the Somme.
Passchendaele's heroes remembered with pride, while Belfast's
young soldiers are pushed to one side.
But if Eton's green fields won brave Waterloo
Then the Falklands and Gulf owe Belfast their due.

For you send your young men off, no reason of why and they
learn quick in Belfast for fear that they'll die.
And they come home as soldiers, baptised under fire
Yet no war exists says the Governments liar.

But a war surely is there, one day it will cease
And the people on both sides will live long in peace
And the blood of the soldier will be washed away,
Recalled once a year, on Remembrance Day.

But for now life goes on in the city's heartbeat.
And soldiers, well, we're still deployed on the street.
And no one is shocked when the headline is cried,
"In Belfast last night, another soldier died..."

1983

Latharna's Race

Green hills that back a special place,
The homeland of Latharna's race.
With Inver running through her core,
To harbour mouth and tower on shore.
A brae where scholar's minds are fed,
Her hill where golfers used to tread.
The market square and thronged Main Street,
That curving sickle, to Olderfleet.

Three chimneys seen from distant heights,
A factory large that lit the nights.
The Mourne, the Pye, the Paper Mill,
In my mind's eye I see them still.
The Steel and Sons an annual rite,
No other team put up a fight.
B League was ours, just hand it over,
Our Inver Park, a field in clover.

Latharna, Eagle, the Hi, the Lo,
McNeills, King's Arms, where did they go?
Cosy snugs, smoke laden air,
Great craic we had when on the tear.
All gone and more as times got bad,
Barnhill forlorn, the mood so sad.
Main Street blocked off, bomb scares and fear,
So many Larne Yins, left from here.

To find the life they knew was there,
A fresh new start, but hard to bear.
To leave the home so deep ingrained,
A new path trod, but each step pained.
And this was not the first nor last,
For émigrés as much our past
As Chaine and Smiley, Drumalis, Moyle,
And so they left, for foreign soil.

But times have changed and spirits soar,
To see our Town revived once more.
Aye, yet we still will moan and gripe,
And at the council, take a swipe.
For being eejits with what they say,
For building bandstands in Broadway.
But credit due to those that serve,
For most of us would have no nerve.

So, here's to them and our wee Town,
A snake in a park we helter down.
Dulse thronged rocks where we slip and fall,
The Maidens' lights, that foghorn's call.
Town hall with clock and Gardenmore,
The promenade, our gorgeous shore,
Playing fields and Sandy bay,
All of these still here today.

All in a Town with civic pride,
That grieved so hard when many died
In January, Fifty-three,
When lost so many to the sea.
Oh, yes, our wee town's tough, it's true,
We've lost some things that we may rue.
But at its heart the town stands strong,
Because it's home… Where we belong.

And when old Sam* with paints in hand,
Expressed the beauty of our land
He also caught a past so bold,
Our home,
Where once Latharna strolled.

* Sam McLarnon (1923-2012) was a prolific and outstanding Larne Watercolourist.

Life's Gallery

We are artwork along the passageways of others.
Illustrating life, darkening mood, illuminating contentment.
Bright kaleidoscopes of love and sorrow, pain and passion.

Moving from earth to earth, take the chance to stop and study.
It is always worthwhile.
Always.

But time is too quickly gone to gaze, transfixed on images that rip our soul.
I've loved the art I shared and hated parting with masterpieces.
Yet life is richer for the encounter.
Always.

Love And Romance Never Ends

On Valentine's I sat bereft, no postie's knock for me
The cards I saw in Harry's shop, would wave quite scornfully

No chance of heart pace quickening, no chance of love returned
No mission of bold stepping out, just fear of being spurned

And yet with furtive gaze I knew, the envelope's great code
The sequence of the letters, the meanings they foretold

I knew that kisses sealed such things, in passion lovingly
And CHIPS and FISH made fairly sure he'd not be home for tea!

And yet the one that made me smile when it was written down
Was that simple run of letters, spelling out my native town.

Oh who had been that Shakespeare? The poet of their day
Who figured out that plain old SWALK could never clearly say

What dear old LARNE would shout aloud, for teenage hearts to swear
Those five wee words so easy spoke, in love, when all is fair.

Lover's Smile

I've written poems, I've sighed at night
Languid, I scaled the stairs
I've prayed to God for help in life
To lighten all my cares

And now I write another verse
To remind myself, things could be worse
For now I see that which I sought
With fortunes yet could not be bought

Contentment is the price to gain
Survive the ride, outlast the pain
I know a joy will visit here
I pray I overcome the fear

To take on life and do one's best
To build again, withstand the test
For no one has the right to quit
The least of us should struggle yet

Life is a gift we're lent to try
A thought to touch, a breath to cry
A swirling mix of love and rage
Scattered dreams upon a page

And when I end my final day
Should a lover pass this way
And stop to think a tender while
I pray my life evokes a smile.

Make It Royal

There is a place in Wiltshire
that was known to a few.
Until their response to a country's loss
proved loyal, strong and true.
They line their streets more often
than any would have thought.
To focus the attention
on a freedom dearly bought
in Kandahar and Helmand
in that far off distant land
that Kipling knew and wrote about
so Tommy would understand.

But no-one thought that we would ever
have to go again.
Until that autumn morning
when we felt our cousin's pain.
As the towers were raped and kindled
in the wrath of burning hate
we knew the world had changed that day
and war was now our fate.
That our youngest men and women
would be called upon to serve.
That our nation would be tested
and we'd have to hold our nerve.

But an eight year trial was not a term
envisaged to be borne.
That the life blood of our Forces
would be scattered, shot and torn.
That foreign fields would take the best
that we would send their way.
That we'd watch the Lyneham hearses
flying home day after day.

And so we felt fatigued by war,
frustrated by the cost.
The fallen of Afghanistan,
bodies injured, maimed, lives lost.
Then Wootton Bassett reminded us
that we must pay our dues.
Regardless of our politics,
our feelings or our views.

So thank you to the Wiltshire town
for standing in our name.
To herald all the fallen
with no care for rank or fame.
A silent tribute, simply paid
to those that had to die.
Your time and care so precious
as each coffin passes by.

2010

Mark Armstrong, Private 1319, 13th Battalion, East Yorkshire Regiment

I walk no longer midst men or mud,
I should be grateful.
For both were clinging, torturous, pitiful,
Neither did me good.
Sucking clay, deep, feet deep, knee deep.
Clogging every waking moment,
Boots weighing a hundredweight,
Clothes wet, mired, dried, mired and dried,
Brittle.

Keen men, scared, bravely scared.
Wallowing in fear on sleepless nights,
Nerves, pulling down like lead weights,
Tears hidden, dried on muddy sleeves, minds fraught, taut,
Brittle.

Then my peace delivered. A flash,
A mighty flash, no noise, yet as I spun I knew.
My world turned slate grey and brown over and over, I knew.
I watched, interested as mud reached up, enveloping me
With the small hands of my precious boys,
Who went before and now guide their father.

In the aftermath of man's insanity.
I shall lie torn asunder in mud. Unknown.
For my King and country, my comrades, my family and you,
Men, women yet unborn,
Your future bought with my blood.

In mud.

Multitudes of Indifference

I tried to look her in the eye
My effort buckled, defeated
Undone by youthful grief,
Etched deeper than her years
Holding bleakness, sealed fate, shortened future.

I looked down
A thin blanket, wrapped pathetically,
Pulled tight, stretching each shredded gap,
No barrier to fingers of wind, searching for weakness.
Their damp wetness prodding into blanket, clothes, soul.
Unerring, grasping, freezing
All to an unforgiving pavement.

I looked away
Thoughts unbidden, wondered,
If I gave money, in answer to a timid palm,
Balanced precariously on the edge of a knee,
On the edge of a life.
Would it fuel a habit, relentless?
Or is this thought, this wonder, not unbidden?
Is it subliminally placed by an uncaring media?
Lulling, cajoling, terrifying me into banal oblivion?
Shall my humanity overcome my hostility, my hopelessness?
I can't make a difference, provide a base
A job, a toe-hold, a house, a family, love
My kindness tries to crush angry selfishness
And fails.
I know I can't do it all,
So I do nothing.

I looked to her eyes
Which stared back, then dropped their gaze
Knowing I would do nothing
A palm turned, cupping knees, drawing up in defence

Protection from a passing multitude of indifference
Which includes me
Smiling weakly, I bar my conscience from screaming.

I looked up
An impassioned hoarding, implores me to buy
A proof of success
Drive my ego in secure luxury
For a bargain price,
Enough to rent a room
For a year.

I look back, briefly.
She is huddled as my guilt huddles,
Shamefully pushing the face and crumpled figure out
Away from a mind that grows angry.
I never wished this on her.
It's not my fault, she is a victim.
Her circumstances, contriving against her, not me.
Not my problem.
Bitterness bullies her into a suitable corner of a material mind.

And so, I look forward
Pulling my heavy coat close, boarding a train, to home
To firm doors and tight windows, to warming drinks.

I look to the glass
Yet as I sip I am distracted
By the face of a girl, shivering
On the whim of a cold, violent city.
Solemnly I pray she survives, God grant her dreams
And in your glory, relieve me of my responsibility
Allow me to pass my humanity to your omnipresence.
For you can solve this, not I
And with a simple prayer
I crush any reason to care
It lets me sleep
And she dies in my mind's eye.

Next Time

I remember hugging you
there, happy, strong
your laughter
your smile
waving from the step
till next time.

Next time.

My hand on your shoulder
smiling down
your face calm
still, soft, silent
till next time.

Next time.

Lifting you up
shared weight
yet no weight
lowering you
casting earth
on wood
till next time.

Next time.

Tracing letters
admiring stone
listening, quiet
hearing your laughter
feeling your hug
no next time.

One Sun

My world turns away
With 28's* twittering
In a breeze of lushness
Longer shadows
Reaching fingers of twilight
Into my soul
Caressing my mind
To soft sleep

* An onomatopoeic name for the Australian Ringneck Parrot.

Occasions

Occasionally you just need someone to be there
Not to talk or even to listen
Just to be
Just to watch the tear fall slowly and not comment
Merely understand.

Occasionally you need a shoulder to rest upon
And feel the warmth of the world returned
The person whom fate positions
Steals a memory
And locks it in your heart
To last forever
Bringing smiles when brought to mind.

And should occasion arise,
That life plays fickle carer to your comfort
Know a memory will cause me
To bring a smile
To be there for you.

Parallels

Time itself is a stranger to the passage of my shadow.

I walk in places that I have left behind.
I look across a ribbon and see myself
A distant figure in parallel tracks;

Perhaps the world revolves in spirals.

Poppy Wreaths Are Laid

I left to serve with happy heart,
no thoughts of death or fear,
I even smiled and thought to tease, my Mother's silent tear.

"Don't worry Mother, dry your eyes and wish me all your best.
For Kaiser Bill will scamper quick, when Pals he tries to test.
We'll sweep him up and throw him out of Flanders bonny fields.
For God is with the righteous; his glory as our shields.
I'll be right back afore you know, your tears will hardly fall,
So see me off, with one more hug, for I answer duty's call."

A warm farewell from cheering crowds and bands of fife and drum.
So soon to France and trenches, and cold that made me numb.
With whizzbang shells and sniper fire,
my happiness soon ebbed.
For nothing saps your spirits,
like rats gnawing on the dead.

The winter turned to mud and snow,
some died from it alone.
No silent night this Christmas,
the war had changed its tone.
No honour left 'tween Fritz and us,
no truce to play a game.
Our only goal, to kill them all,
for they're the ones to blame.

Then the push to end it, how true that was for me.
I got twelve yards with stumbled steps and didn't even see,
the bullets cutting like a swathe,
my guts all ripped to hell.
No pain, no sound, no screaming cries,
no tolling of a bell.

My face in mud, my breath all gone,
a darkness then a light.
I know I'm dead, yet am back home,
my Mother in my sight.
Her tears are falling hard and fast,
a bugle call is played.
A silence falls around the town.
Then poppy wreaths are laid.

My perch on high, unbounded force,
affords a spirit's view.
I think some years have flown past,
I'm sure it is a few.
No more my pals who made it home,
seem to gather here.

No more can I see Mother,
no more her silent tear.
Yet now some others march instead.
Old men who were not born,
when I went forward into death,
my young life ripped and torn.

And though no wreath that's laid this day, restores my life to me,
Each allows my soul to rest, held safe in memory.

Princess Victoria
(Women and Children First)

No screams
Save for us,
Who were left on shore

No tears
Save for the men
Who found the shore

But noise, massive noise
Souls torn,
Gales ripping
Jarred nerves
Radios shrieking
Heralds of disaster

A town scarred
Never forgetting
Nor her sister on the other shore

That day
When gallant actions
So long in our nature
Killed so many

Revolve

Does the world revolve in spirals?
Drifting corkscrewed through our time?
Do I walk still where I lingered?
Do you see me in your mind?

Each and every day I wonder
Effortless, though still with pain
Ego causes doubt and worry
Early life was much the same

As I walk along the one road
Another I walked different paths
A parallel that I can sense there
And wish to see the I to ask

Tell me is the path that I chose
Those decisions that I made
Turns performed and options taken
This my life, was it ordained?

Hollow now my thoughts and motives
How I loved and how I died
Hallowed ground my resting place now
Hope you came; I hope you cried.

River Paths

As rivers flow their paths to sea
I must follow the source of me
That which drives my heart and soul
That which is my life's true goal

Time is swift and unforgiving
A passion needed for the living
Or drift and laze my life away
With no real change in every day

To roll ideas around my head
To live the dream to which I'm led
To wonder thoughts of new direction
That I can take and find perfection

So now I set my path to take
The joyous walk for my soul's sake
The life that truly is for me
As rivers flow their paths to sea.

Self-Reflections

Another year has passed away
Yet look at you, no hairs of grey
Or if there are I cannot see
For you are beautiful to me

The year that's gone was not so bad
You made it through, for that be glad
The diet maybe not so much
The fitness plan, just out of touch

But be not down upon yourself
You've got your looks, you've got your health
Your wit and charm, incisive mind
All still sharp, I really find
That as I look upon your face
In this reflection I must chase
The modesty that stays my hand

From telling me

"I'm doing grand."

Southern Santa

In the spirit of Christmas, I should write a verse
But that seems quite cheesy, and possibly worse,
It would have to be festive and full of good cheer
When to be truthfully honest, I'd rather not hear
Of Santa and reindeers, of holly and snow
The trimmings and turkey, the cattle laid low.

I'd rather just sit with a glass in my hand
And wiggle my toes in the heat of the sand
For I'm in Australia and it's bloody hot
The middle of winter, it's certainly not.
Today it was forty, no wind, not a breeze
But cards from afar continue to tease
With Dickensian urchins, wrapped up in the snow
This warped view of Yuletide is all that we know.

Yet it turns out a white one is not out of reach
For the sand it is gleaming, down here on the beach
The beer is so cold and the food quite sublime
So perhaps it's okay to write my own rhyme

To wish you good cheer from the sunshine so bright
A Merry Oz Christmas, joy to all, she'll be right.

Sunday Mornings

Cold pizza on a bedroom floor
Head dull, mouth rank, tongue tobacco tingled.
Sunlight, obnoxiously bright, illuminates debris.
Eyes crack open, gazing upon majestically withered olives, rubber cheese
And little brown bits,
That might be mushrooms.
I hope.
Lie still, eyes shut, waiting for room to catch up.

Recall the night, patchy.
Early doors okay, see it all in Technicolor.
Later stages, jumpy pictures, missing reels.
Laughs and jokes with best of friends
Trouble in street, punches ducked, landed, received, given.

Ran them out of Dodge, taken flight.
Blanks, more gaps then spicy pizza.
"Chillies, best and hottest you have my good man."
Stupid boast and laughter; crying hurt from heat.
Stumble into street, fleeting girl in grasp.
Where did she come from, what was her name?

Morning eases into focus, mind steadier, stable room.
Think of Sunday's plans
Breakfast meetings, lads, pub, big screen, match.
First order; three Ss, then on the road, out the door.
Time to move.
Yawn and stretch and what the…

Who is she?

The Fall

Autumnal worries make my life
Such a mismatch of colourful irony springing
Ideas and ideals.
Hesitant, light green but soon
Vibrant in youthful confidence.
Needing to twist and turn and grow and live.
In sunlight and occasional showers
Warmed and cooled, succoured and sustained.

To glorious deep bottle green, bathed in sun and heat,
Warmth, light, long hours and days
That would never, ever end. My life's goal
Fulfilled, complete, harvesting the means to live for ever.
Passing on my rich cargo, synthesising
For the wonder, majesty and strength
That I stem from.
Then the sun dipped, days foreshortened
My life an irony of vibrancy.
Colours never to be equalled,
Colours to be envious of, revelled in,
Dreamt of, worshipped.
Ironically, in my death throes I become my most beautiful and so
I have waited.
Until now.
A gentle breeze and my fall.
Twisting, turning, floating
A fall within the Fall.
To end until I can once more be brought up
Through roots, reborn.
The joy in knowing silence for the snows.

The Nine

The Queen of arable beauty
in majesty reaches to the sea.
Where the waves of passing currents
pay homage to her radiance.
Eight siblings lie beside her,
each in their way stunning.
Her brother's army marshalled in the south
and her youngest sister skipping to the north.
Sorrowful death in their midst.
But happiness and beauty are the family traits.

The melodies of their history reach far and near.
While the Diaspora who claim them as home
look backward, ever backward.
Their longings filled with images
of cottage fires and deep green hues,
trees with entwined initials.
Timeless, glacial carvings that beckon still.
Seeing them in my mind.
Needing them in my soul.
The bejewelled, unsullied, legendary nine.

There's Something Not Right With My Tummy

There's something not right with my tummy
I'm running all day to the loo
I'm feeling all queasy and funny
I'm not really sure what to do.

So I asked my young man for assistance
To guess what the matter might be
He said that it really was simple;
It's the coffee and lager and tea!

So I cut down on all of my drinking
But the feeling did not go away.
I decided to book an appointment
To hear what the doctor would say.

He looked at my tongue, my stomach and bum
My ears, my nose and my feet
And then with a glee, which I plainly see
He asked me to *"Please take a seat"*.
There's everything right with my tummy.
The doctor he tells me with pride
That he's just had the privilege of hearing
The heartbeat, of my baby inside.

View From A Bus Window

Casually confident footpath walker
Intelligent face, calm.
Corporate man with half-smile, picking his corporate way
Midst the flow and eddies of office workers, shop assistants,
school girls.
All whirled and pulled by the Maccers on the corner.
He's aiming for the pedestrian crossing
Avoiding the corporate feast machine
When he bumps into a dam.

I'm just remotely observing
My bus window framing the scene.
I see the moment
When his kind eyes turn cold.
The intelligent face changes, the half-smile frozen,
Confidence draining, eyes darting, furtively
To anywhere.
Just not back to what he has seen
Alas, too late. The dam is moving.

Trainers, faded blue jeans, un-tucked shirt.
One hand out, fingers extended.
One thrust deep into pocket.
Shoulders hunched, head tilted
A submissive. No threat.
But a dam nonetheless.
A block.
Our corporate man attacks.

I read his smooth lips, *"No, thank you."*
Said to the air.
No eye contact with the dam.
Just no, thank you.

But so clear and precise
That he, under the proscenium arch of my bus window theatre
can be read.
His lips pronounce it.

The dam watches him closely.
Anticipates the move.
The side-step to pass by.
But does nothing to block or pursue
Corporate man, makes the safety of the crossing.
Confidence returning, half-smile reattached.
Plunging back into the safety of eddies and flows.

The hunched shoulders turn to wait for the next passer-by
Hoping that they won't.

My bus dawdled, waiting for an encore performance.
Lights holding their red spotlight to the world.

I watched the oncoming tide.
Tried to judge the moment they saw him.
When their eyes changed, diverted, their faces set
The hurried shake of head
Or mumbled *"No"*
The complete change in direction for the meek.

As different as the races of Man
They all shared a look.
Of hunted animals.
Yet he was always submissive.
In his every movement, his every approach.
But they saw what they perceived.
Shying away from him like gazelle.

I noticed his haircut.
Precise.
Neat, short, square cut on the neck, tidy.
Newly done.

I wondered.
A beggar with neat hair.
So I looked closer.
His trainers, not shabby, clean.
Faded jeans, but so were mine
Un-tucked shirt, yet ironed.
Precisely.

Then my bus moved on
The tableau of the city
Left far behind in green effects
And I wondered about it.

I still do.

Waving Goodbye

She stood at the window her little hand waving
She stood at the window just waving goodbye
I lifted her up so she could see clearly
And answered her question
When she asked me why
Your Daddy's a soldier, he must do his duty
Your Daddy's a soldier, he leaves as he must
But he will come back love, to hold and to hug you
He will come back
From the heat and the dust

You've been there before love like many another
You've been there before and you've always come home
So promise me now my beautiful soldier
Promise me this is the last time you'll roam

We turned from the window as you walked away love
We turned from the window and got on with our lives
And you and your comrades are fighting for freedom
While waiting at home are the children and wives

The media rallies the hopes of a nation
The media rallies for the sake of our boys
And leaders in suits tell us all this is vital
While our breaking hearts are lost in the noise

My thoughts always drift to the day I first met you
My thoughts always drift to the love that I felt
Your smile and your laughter, your confident bearing
It all worked its magic and made my heart melt
A whirlwind romance that most people doubted
A whirlwind romance, an engagement, a ring
While family and friends tried to caution against it
We stuck to our plans and eloped in the spring

We were so happy, just our love between us
We were so happy though oft times apart
For the Army would send you to far distant places
But I always knew
You had me in your heart

I never imagined a happiness greater
I never imagined our love could be more
But then came our daughter, and we gazed at her being
The love flowed around us, I felt my heart soar

As you go away now each time it is harder
As you go away now her little heart aches
And I feel her sorrow as I watch her tears falling
Her sadness and longing just makes my heart break.
We fill our alone time and she talks about Daddy
We fill our alone time so she's happy and bright
I never allow her to see that I worry
Yet I think that she hears
My sobbing at night

A knock at the door and my heart leaps so frightened
A knock at the door, my world shatters like glass
The uniformed figures I see on the doorstep
Are Death's chosen heralds, they've found me at last
I hear they are talking but words just wash over
I hear they are talking but my soul's deep in pain
For I know I have lost you to an enemy's bullet
I never will hold you
In my arms again

The cortege is passing the flag drapes your coffin
The cortege is passing, she's waving goodbye
She stands by my side, her little hand waving
And I give her no answer
When she asks me why.

Weekday Jam

Frustrating circle in endless loop
Refutes all attempts at progress.
Terry chats, gentle brogue soothing
My rising annoyance stayed by a curling smile.
Airborne ridiculousness makes the morning flow
Smoothly, unlike the metal scrap yard positioned round our city.

I ease my right foot down, left foot up
Balancing finesse to inch forward
Small movement, small comfort.
My wandering mind counts the time
Minutes and hours stretching into the distance of my past
Numbers that total one day every month, wasted
In tedious waiting.

And so I left it all behind.
Living now where five cars at a light is a hold up.
Delays of five minutes, a major crisis.
No jams, except Vegemite.
I'm just jammy I guess.
But I miss Terry.

Wind In City Valleys

Nature's leaf blower, umbrella turner, skirt raiser
Hair dryer, flag wrapper
Stormy autumnal golden debris cascades on black rivers
Slamming passers-by, bending forward struggling
Tottering on grey banks
Joyful children hair fuzzled,
Windmill gripping
Extended arms, leaning forward giggling
Roguishly held by imagination, skydivers, wind surfers
Calmness brings an end to their games.

What Do You Get A Chihuahua For Christmas?

What do you get a Chihuahua for Christmas?
Or is that not a thing one should do?
Will the Mexican pedigree simper?
And be really quite pissed off at you?

Will the assumption that Spanish means Christian
And the fact that the pooch doesn't care
Mean that all of your efforts are wasted?
And surely that's probably fair

For no dog should be this subjected
To the vagaries of owners so crass
That they think a wee dog needs a present
When the dog would just much rather pass

For the dog needs no trimmings or crackers
It just needs the love from yourself
But let all of those facts be discarded
And dress the wee dog as an elf

Then post it on Facebook and Twitter
Instagram obviously too
And be glad that Chihuahuas are doggies
Who can't hire lawyers to sue.

About the Author

Ian was born in Northern Ireland in 1966. At eighteen, he joined the Royal Air Force. Throughout his Service he had the pleasure of working alongside some "right eejits" that he still feels lucky to call friends. On leaving the Service he relocated to Western Australia and is now surrounded by a resident mob of Kangaroos who bounce past his house each day. They remind him of his previous colleagues.

He is the author of *A Time To Every Purpose,* an alternative history novel with a religious twist, the '*Wright & Tran*' series of crime thrillers, as well as *Slaughtered Nursery Rhymes for Grown Ups, Self-Publishing for Independent Authors* and a few other titles that he contributed to as a ghost writer.

He currently hosts the Book Reality YouTube and Podcast channels. (Come subscribe and make him very happy!)

"In a market inundated with so many books, it is a relief to find an author who is more than just the sum total of his attributes – there is something prodigious, an elusive extra that makes Ian Andrew's work special. It also helps that [he is] blessed with quite exceptional story-telling skills. Andrew delivers adrenalin and excitement laced with imaginative, innovative technology with memorable characters who provide heart and substance to his work." (Elaine Fry – The West Australian)

Extras

Come visit www.bookreality.com
or email Ian at ian@leschenaultpress.com

By Ian Andrew

A Time To Every Purpose

Leigh Wilson, the preeminent scientist of her generation, has invented a way to look back into time. Banned from using it for anything more than investigative purposes by a brutal regime that fears its power, she complies in the face of insurmountable odds. But the world is changing and in the aftermath of a vicious murder Leigh now faces her ultimate dilemma. Can she muster the courage to act and reset her reality?

A Time to Every Purpose is a fast moving thriller with amazing twists and turns that grips you through to its final, unexpected climax. A ground-breaking, cross-genre thriller from an exciting author.

"A Time To Every Purpose by Ian Andrew deals with huge concepts, looking at the broad sweep of history… a well-executed alternate history novel with some great action scenes."

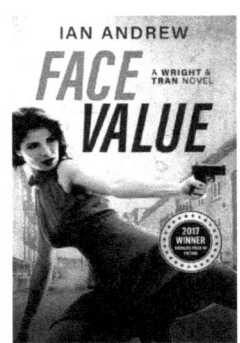

Face Value

Kara Wright and Tien Tran, former members of an elite intelligence gathering team active in Afghanistan, Iraq, and places still classified, now make their living through Wright & Tran, a PI service that tracks errant spouses, identifies dishonest employees and, just occasionally, takes on more significant cases that allow them to use all their skills.

When siblings Zoe and Michael Sterling insist that their middle-aged parents have gone missing, Kara and Tien are at first sceptical and then quickly intrigued; the father, ex-intelligence analyst Chris Sterling, appears to be involved with an enigmatic Russian thug.

Using less than orthodox methods and the services of ex-colleagues with highly specialised talents, Wright & Tran take on the case. But the truth they uncover is far from simple and will shake Zoe and Michael as much as it will challenge Tien and anger Kara. Anger she can ill afford for she is being hunted by others for the killing of a street predator who chose the wrong prey.

The only constant in this darkening world is that nothing and no one can be taken at face value.

Flight Path

Wright & Tran are back!

Kara Wright and Tien Tran, combat veterans of an elite intelligence unit, now make their living as Private Investigators. Often working the mundane, just occasionally they get to use all their former training.

"I'd like you to make sure the dead are really dead."

So it is that the enigmatic Franklyn tasks Kara and Tien to investigate the apparent suicide of a local celebrity. Within days the women are embarked on a pursuit that leads halfway around the globe and into the darkest recesses of the human condition. Kara, Tien and their team will endure mental stress worse than anything they experienced from combat and, like combat, not everyone makes it home.

Also out now: Fall Guys (Book 3 in the Wright & Tran Series)

www.ingramcontent.com/pod-product-compliance
Lightning Source LLC
Chambersburg PA
CBHW072107110526
44590CB00018B/3352